WHISK OF DUST

SHERMAN KENNON

CONTENTS

SERENITY

A wandering star breathing life into a desolate night.

The wind racing across the sky,

stirring the leaves of trees as it passes by.

Misty rain appearing from nowhere in sight.

Calming the skies as dark gives way to light.

As too ceasing tension of an aggravated night.

A seed planted patiently in a row

as patiently waiting for it to grow.

Rain dancing upon the roof,

orchestrating a melody appeasing to the soul.

Every drop pure as precious gold.

MOMENTS

A silent breeze swept away a moment,

one that never can be recaptured,

never can it be relived.

So it is for us to cherish the moments,

cherish them with all of our might.

For just as an eagle in flight,

they are transient,

soon vanishing like the moon as day return the light.

Soon they are but a memory,

swiftly escaping just as the wind flowing through the star filled night.

When they're gone you wish to still hold on.

So it is for us to cherish the moments,

cherish them with all of our might,

for soon they are gone just as the day will replace the night.

WHISK OF DUST

From the African terrains,

stirred of a mere whisk of dust,

transcended into the midst of the Caribbean.

Alighted upon a new land.

Still,

as a motionless night,

graceful as an eagle in flight.

Too unseen distance,

finding little peace,

but much uproar and the presence of war.

The one earth shaken at the hands of man,

but remaining strong,

"being braced by the arms of God."

To supply and multiply,

to enrich its inhabits well being,

that we all shall live prosperous and be free.

COGITATIONS

A shadeless tree longing for the blooming coming with spring,

glittering of beauty for all to see.

A river that flows,

stretching into the ocean,

from here to beyond on and on it flows,

graceful with every motion.

A mystical rain calming a boisterous night.

A sensuous breeze sending leaves into flight.

A beautiful flower reminding one of a more treasured hour.

A wandering mind wanting for a better world,

if only it had the power.

A time to think,

a time to act.

A time to stand,

a time to react.

A time to speak,

a time for silence.

A time for peace,

time to stop the violence.

SEARCH

"I struggle through the dark

in search of the light.

I sometimes want to give up

but realize that winning means continuing to fight.

Often I'm considered wrong

even when I've proven myself right,

sometimes told to just give up and accept the loss,

but victory is very much in my sight."

FLOW

"By the water that flow calmly,

a breeze that blow thinking or maybe wondering where for does it go?

Beneath hold life abundant of many perhaps never seen but too of his great creation.

So one will believe if belief is in what is seen

or maybe not seen,

true it is there as true as time will pass,

never too stand still.

Each moment embrace or more so cherish.

As gentle the wind blows,"

"wrap yourself within its flow."

You Are

"At times I know that I act childish and immature,

I sometimes question why you choose to endure.

Please know that at times,

the words I cannot find.

It is my hope that this verse will reveal a few things from this sometimes wondering mind.

Perhaps I am not sure just who I am,

but if I am a flower,

you are the water that enables me to grow.

If I am a door,

you are the key that allows passage.

If I am an ocean,

you are the content that gives me reason to exist."

"If I am nothing,

it is because of me,

but my desire to excel and accomplish many things,

perhaps it is because of you."

THE ANSWER

"Will there be peace?

Will there be love?

Must there be war?

Why is there so much hate?

In my heart I long for this peace,

but through my eyes I see this war,

my heart feels this love,

but my soul aches from this hate.

So many questions.

Many try to render the answer,

but there is only one answer,

it is the same answer now that it was in beginning.

Until we all realize that answer,

there will be war.

Until we understand that there is only one answer,

there will be hate."

"Will the day come that we all understand that no matter the question,

God is the answer?"

THE LIGHT

"You turned to the left,

but your destination was to the right.

You searched for the stars,

then realized it was day and not night.

You went in search of peace,

but everyone you encountered had a desire to fight.

Many questioned why you continued moving forward.

I can only imagine it was because at the end of the tunnel,

you could see the light."

Focus

"I chase the stars and wonder where they lead.

I follow the wind in search of the calm that follows.

I sometimes seek shelter from the rain.

Other times I relish the moisture that it brings.

I enjoy the cold of winter but find myself longing for the heat of summer.

I gaze at the moon,

and I'm fascinated by the stars.

I love being free.

I cringe at the thought of being confined."

"My mind sometimes wonders,

but my focus remains clear."

WE RISE

Treacherous mountains to climb,

harsh valleys to cross.

But brighter days will come just as the morning,

ever shining bright transforming darkness into light.

Just as dust of a gentle breeze,

quiet ascends of fallen leaves,

upward to the skies.

Still,

we rise.

YOUR BEAUTY

"As darkness falls across the star filled sky

I gaze motionless into your eyes

and ultimately I'm forced into a natural high.

My heart pounds at the pace of an African drum

I began to question my own vision

Can such beauty really exist?

With great speed my mind began searching

I search for words that might express your beauty

I think of great and total also comes to mind

I even ponder absolute,

but these are not enough,

so the words still I cannot find.

Perhaps my search is in vain"

"Maybe there are no words

powerful enough for me to explain,

yet I continue searching

I search for the words that might express" your beauty.

Nothing Else

"Indeed it is love,

for nothing else can be so pure,

nothing brings such happiness,

of nothing else have I felt so sure.

There are things I can do without,

things that leave much doubt,

but what I am sure of is the essence of your love.

My heart I open,

allowing my love to connect with yours.

We join together and trust that our love lasts forever.

Indeed it is love,

for nothing else can be so pure."

This Dance

"May I have this dance

that I might hold you tight?

I wish for this song to last forever

that I might hold you through the night.

I've always enjoyed this song

but never as much as now.

I softly sing along

as a harmonizing whisper gently in your ear.

I can't remember you more beautiful

than you are right now,

my love.

May I have this dance

that I might hold you through

The night?

A Closer Look

Things are sometimes faded

but they will always become clear,

where there seems nothing but bad,

look closer,

you're sure to find good,

when you've tried and there seems no hope,

find strength from within and try once again,

when others give in and assure you there's no way,

rest mind,

body,

and soul and know tomorrow starts a new day,

and if you're blessed to see that day,

embrace and use it in a positive way."

Unyielding

I grasp for things I cannot see.

I long for power I cannot have.

I wait for that which never come.

I call out to that which does not exist.

I lay in hope of rest.

I strive in spite of rejection.

I hunger for more of what is good.

I strive for peace and love.

I fight resistance from every direction.

I'm told things will never change,

but I'm determined to make a difference."

THIS LOVE

Today is a special day,

for this day,

we celebrate our love.

Yesterday was also special,

for we celebrated our love.

It is a love that no other can claim.

There are none who can understand its depths,

none who would realize its true power.

Tomorrow,

we will celebrate our love,

and every day thereafter,

we will celebrate this love,

for it is a love that has no end."

QUIETUDE

Sunlight shines beauty aglow,

by the banks of the river that quietly flow.

Misty rain yields comfort to a muggy night.

Wind of a gentle breeze,

calming the skies destine of rendering light.

CHASE THE WIND

"I chase the wind and get lost in the clouds.

I'm sweep into darkness in my search for the light.

I see the future but get caught up in the past.

I strive for first.

It sure beats coming in last.

Still I chase the wind and float as a gentle breeze up among the stars

then descending as a bird down amidst the trees."

"Still I chase the wind,

gradually gaining

yet never gaining.

Still forever,

I chase the wind."

FAMILY

"There are many things in our lives that we hold dear.

But nothing can take the place of having family near.

The times we get together are sometimes far and apart.

But that makes the time we're together more enduring to our hearts.

Family is like a tree that bears many fruit.

It's sometimes damaged by the storms.

But remains strong because of its solid root.

Unlike materialistic things that soon will fade away.

Family is durable,

built to last day after day."

THE BIRTH

"From the top of the hill

Shined the sparkling light,

A light that had shined

All through the night.

People gathered to explore

This unique sight,

They stood all during the morn,

Finally to find that baby Jesus

Was born.

To remember that wonderful day,

I so eagerly say.

It comes but once a year

Packed with such joy and cheer.

It's a time family and friends

Come together,

As do a dove's wings

As it clinches its snowball-white feathers.

It's a time enemies set aside Their fight,

and join together In singing "Silent Night."

"It's a time men,

women,

boys,

and girls

All join together and voice joy to the world.

Yes,

it comes but once a year

So let's all enjoy the Christmas cheer."

Touch the Sky

Touch the sky and fly like an eagle.

Spread your wings and open your heart.

Fill it with love,

then fly away.

Spreading love all over the land.

Covering it as grains of sand.

Touch the sky and fly like an eagle.

Build up dreams,

tear down barriers.

Lift up peace,

eliminate war.

Touch the sky and fly like an eagle.

Eradicate hate that love will prevail.

The Stars

"The stars so bright

bringing life to the dark skies of night.

I reach because they appear so close,

but reality reminds me that they're so far away.

This same distance is that of your touch

for the farther I reach,

the more distant you become.

Voices in my head urge me to leave you alone,

but the desire of my heart reminds me

that I'm not that strong.

I fear that you are as a star,

appearing so close

that I feel I can touch you

but actually being so far away

that I never will."

WITHOUT YOU

"I find it hard to focus

For my mind seems

To always find its way to you.

The nights are restless

The days unfulfilled.

I fear that I'm losing my mind

Slowly going insane.

I'd go to a doctor

But for this they can offer

No cure.

In my heart I know what is true.

There are people all around me.

Many things to see and do.

But I find myself lost without you."

Confused

"The sky was clear

But it rained

With tremendous force.

Trees were still

But wind blew with reckless abandon

It was extremely hot

Yet the temperature fell below freezing.

The ocean was at peace

Yet it raged with a powerful force.

It was early in the afternoon

But somehow dark outside

I was very sure but now I'm left Confused."

STILL A LIE

"A bird is still a bird even if it can no longer fly.

A fish is still a fish even if it loses its ability to swim.

A dog is still a dog even if it never barks.

A tree is still a tree even if it no longer flourishes.

A lie is still a lie even if it's disguised as the truth."